THIS LITTLE WHILE

THE MACMILLAN COMPANY
NEW YORK • BOSTON • CHICAGO
DALLAS • ATLANTA • SAN FRANCISCO

MACMILLAN AND CO., LIMITED
LONDON • BOMBAY • CALCUTTA
MADRAS • MELBOURNE

THE MACMILLAN COMPANY
OF CANADA, LIMITED
TORONTO

THIS LITTLE WHILE

By JOHN W. LYNCH

Author of "A Woman Wrapped in Silence"

WITH PAINTINGS BY
MARGUERITE S. COCKETT

Copy 1

1950

THE MACMILLAN COMPANY · NEW YORK

Some of his disciples said to one another, What does this mean that he is saying to us, After a little while you will see me no longer and again after a little while you will have sight of me. What is this little while he speaks of . . . ?

St. John's Gospel

ILLUSTRATIONS

FACING
PAGE

Be It Done to Me   1

We Have Seen His Star . . . and Are Come to Adore   5

Arise . . . Take the Child and His Mother and Fly into Egypt   9

And Afterward . . . They Returned into Galilee . . . to Nazareth   13

And They Said: Is Not This the Carpenter's Son?   17

Andrew . . . Findeth First His Brother Simon, and Saith to Him . . . We Have Found . . . the Christ   21

For He Was Teaching Them as One Having Authority   27

And Going Into One of the Ships That Was Simon's He Desired Him to Draw Back a Little from the Land   31

The Master Is Come and Calleth for Thee   35

I Say to You, That If These Shall Hold Their Peace, the Stones Will Cry Out   41

And the Word Was Made Flesh and Dwelt Amongst Us   45

Let Him Be Crucified!   57

The Crucifixion   77

Woman, Why Weepest Thou?   83

Ye Men of Galilee, Why Stand You Looking Up . . .?   91

BE IT DONE TO ME

HERE Calvary begins: the press of pain,
The lash, the circled thorns, the nails, the sobs
That shall be wrung of Him, the wounded side,
All loss and restoration in the dark,
Intended time that is to come, all, all
Are here. . . .

                And when the time beats on the Hill
To break our centuries, then when we see . . .
It shall be only what this moment stabs
In her to hide and carry through the years!

This is the seeding, focus, and the gift
Of God so centered on her heart she is a world
Above her world in steadied, ebbless love.

Thrown close about her now old prophecies
Are curving from a past as deep as guilt
To hurl His meanings at a name they long
Had sought in yearning for fulfillment and release.

This is a woman set at enmity
With evil, and the writhing serpent waits
The crushing of her heel! This is a woman
Under prophecy that swings around
And over her, and of her prayer breaks bright
To brilliance in the piercing tongues of fire
That she, the child of David and the womb
Of God, kneels meek before a motherhood,
Gowned and silvered in virginity!

Pressed down around her here the savage earth,
The past, the future, distant destinies,

Our hopes, repeating sorrows of our years,
The gain, defeat, divisions in all men
And angels, all creation cast this weight
Enclosing her who in an instant, in one pause
And halt against returning aeons of the night,
Takes all upon her heart to be her love.

So Gabriel has come and is a gold
Beneath her and a sea of light to lift
Her in a silhouette of majesty
Above him; and the gold of Gabriel,
The light that is a sea, has trembled to a blush
Before her as he tells God's deference
And pleads the cause of Trinity before her will!

"Hail . . . Mary, . . . full of grace, . . . the Lord is
with thee. . . . Blessed art thou among women."

Humbly, humbly in her littleness
She melts to ask how all of this might be,
For humbly, humbly in her littleness
She holds no easy answer in her prayer.

"The Holy Ghost shall come upon thee, and the power of the
Most High shall overshadow thee . . . the Holy that shall
be born of thee . . . shall be called the Son of God."

The hush above our universe and through
Our universe to unedged deeps, unfathomed
And unnamed, where God is Father and the Son
And Holy Spirit in Himself and Love
And One Procession in the endless Mystery. . . .
The hush along the spools of time and past
The stooping stars is as a space kept
Of infinity to hear the sound of her reply!

"Behold the handmaid of the Lord: be it
done to me according to thy word."

2

Swift then the light invisible speeds from her feet,
Runs ringed and urgent to the crest and utterance
Of joy that breaks like song to echo off the wings
Of Seraphim and spins the spiral down
Until creation, freshened in a day
Made new, is glorious and young with Him!

"Be it done to me according to Thy word."

Reversal here, decision that is self
Reversed whirls now the world back, glad again
That Eve has come and wiser men may be,
Not like the gods as in the ancient lie,
But as the God the new Eve gives to birth.

"Be it done to me."

Submission here, responding and accord
Send light out running from the chaste white feet
To flare and circle to the top and pinnacle
Of bliss that spreads and showers endlessly
Her victory, and ours, in one surrendering.

Yet Nazareth that housed this moment felt
No comets burning in the air, no fall
Of mountains crumbling for the end of loss. . . .

Only a village in a quiet plain
Crept on, while a young girl, kneeling and alone,
Returns to Him a voice in hidden choir.

His Bethlehem is here, His holy night,
The straw, the shepherds and the lonely crib,
And afterwards. . . .

His words, and fishermen,
The bread, the roadside well, dead Lazarus,

3

The lepers, names, the harvests, and the hopes,
The word that He alone speaks to forgive. . . .

All these are at this moment sealed in her,
And she is singing of Magnificat!

Who must now also see

That Calvary begins.

WE HAVE SEEN HIS STAR . . . AND
ARE COME TO ADORE

THESE eager men come climbing out of dark
   To trace the crevices, the cloven rocks,
The spaces in the shadows, spurning height,
Defeating distance, stumbling at the stones,
Down crush and hindrance of the precipice,
Through deserts, hills, the menacing affront
Of knotted oaks, to cast themselves straight willed
As gold and frankincense and myrrh,
Beneath the starlight pouring on the place
Where she is . . .

                    Holding God upon her knees!

This is more than pageantry and slow
Procession stately to the mind in small
Remembrance: nor is bare and frugal birth
Here touched by glitter and formalities
Of kings. These men are lonely, and they seek
For light and stare against an alien sky
To find it, and they will not pause, nor cease,
Nor be diverted. Theirs is search . . . and more,
Since reaching Him, they mean a whole consent.
These postulants have tossed a sovereign past
Behind them, while the questions on their speech
Ask only where . . . where is He, for we come!

They asked of Herod. They had verdict all
Jerusalem's too cautious scribes could say:
They heard the name Micheas wrote inspired
Of God on scrolls five hundred years before.
They had their secret: it was Bethlehem!
And then with Herod's suave pretense, his lie
About them, these swift, artless men had need
Of warning in a dream before they guessed
That something less than love could strike this Child.

So now they climb here up the steeps and down
A world that holds them from His face . . . and time
Is bursting to the long epiphany
That shows Him past the shepherds and the temple gates,
Past Joseph and the broken stall, past hiddenness,
Past angel . . . to the broad and breeding earth
That lies in dark beyond His Bethlehem.

We may not hold it as a flaw that time,
Our long, permissive time, has garnered up
The best in us, our homes, our loves, the good
Persuasions to an innocence, our prayer
And roofs and children, lyric memories,
To cherish Bethlehem within a song,
Falling to the solaced, crowded hearth.

Give gifts and speak the kind word once again,
Deck trees, bake new the frosted cake of festival;
Pour wine, weave legend, kindle fire.
All this is worthy. This is Bethlehem,
And she would have it so who bore the Child.

But Bethlehem is not a sentiment,
Nor falls like easy petals to the ground.
His stable lifts above us as a citadel,
High built to guard against the last defeat,
And held against destruction in the huge
Embrace of emptiness. He brings a city
Made for men who had been homeless and alone,
And in His warfare makes a refuge here,
Not for the fugitive, but for the strong.

This is no granite wall cemented of a fear,
A secret cave, a fenced and guarded ground.
His Bethlehem is bold for history to seize
That we may kneel in hope before this Child
Whose weapons are the gathered straws, Whose blow

Is infancy, Whose banner is a star
Pulled from anonymous and distant hosts
Of all the stars to be His Own . . . and ours!

Be silent on His midnight, treasure peace,
Strain close in hungry arms beloved breasts,
Be young again, sing lullaby to years,
All this is worthy: this is Bethlehem.

Yet hearken to the blast His breathing wakes,
The force, the fierce, relentless energy
That the Will of God should be a Child's small hand,
And He be needing Joseph for a name.
This Bethlehem explodes: above the sky
The white swept storm of Him rolls past our race
To thunder down the whine of little fears,
The boastings of the proud. They are undone,
Are smothered in a Child's high, single cry.

Let stories be, the courtesy, the ways
Of homes that touch the yearning in this crib,
The mistletoe, the holly and the gay
Fresh voices sounding to the chilly air.
Spin new romance, let folk tales be recalled.
All this is worthy: this is Bethlehem.

But think not Bethlehem be vague, be lost
To dream, have no geography
Or limits as a town with streets. . . .

This Bethlehem is actual, as real a place
As Hiroshima.
As definite as bones at Nagasaki,
More circumspect an area of ground
Than western deserts where a bomb's experiment
Cast men upon their stomachs miles away
To tremble in the light they had unlocked,

7

The blind light hidden in the metal's core,
Now flared and searing in the chosen death
That comes to make our rich and vineyard earth
As chalked and cratered as the barren moon!
This Bethlehem is actual, as real a place
As Hiroshima.

And it stands, our Bethlehem, our citadel,
Our gleaming star defensive at His birth,
Our Bethlehem still stands.

"For the world was made by Him, and He was in the world,
In Him was life,
And life was the light of men.
And the light shineth in the darkness. . . ."

ARISE . . . TAKE THE CHILD AND HIS
MOTHER AND FLY INTO EGYPT

H ERE is hatred's failure, cruelty's defeat,
  The ultimate, humiliating lack
That lurks in sublety's considered plan
Of taking thought lest innocence avail
Against invasion, and that truth thereby
Be lessened in its stature by a single cubit.

This is the vale of last impossibles,
The lonely cleft, the unexpected path
To loose His purpose, the uncounted fact
Of corridor that comes not to an end.

And they are hastened on its scar across our world
While Herod's huntsmen slay the lambs of Bethlehem.

He, Herod, should have netted them. There was no fault
Within his reasoning. This was a Child
New born, His parents' residence lay well
Beneath the jurisdiction of the swords.
This Lamb should now be numbered in the slain:
Except that Herod was not Pilate, and his dreams
Encompassed not confessions of a far centurion.

They hasten onward, and their figures bend
With fear impelled by love that would enwrap
Him in their fairer firmament and warmer world.
They feel not huge above Him, gianted
In strength and adequate to Him they hold.
They run away: they turn from Israel
To seek the strangeness of unhallowed Egypt
In swift obedience that is for Him
Creation of the world that they would give.

They pose no armory, no staff, no shield
Deflecting fears in this defenceless flight,

But move here, hiding God, when all His panoply
Is made of the woven garment of her prayer,
And is a man's back bowed like granite cliffs
He envies for the shoulders of their hills.

And yet their love put fear beneath these hills,
Made menaces of shadows, saw the trees
Behind them as pursuers, heard the hooves
Of horses in each echo, changed the twigs to foes,
And mobilized the very ground they trod
To ranks and regiments of Herod-men. . . .

They are in exile, cast from cities, torn
From home, denied, expelled beneath a scorn
And edict where the anguish of a future thins
Their narrowed sky to slash at them the first
Perception of the answers He will find.

The earth has tipped now, pitched them like unwanted skulls
Beyond a desert place. They are the hunted.
Hounds and clubs and lash and law leap near.
They feel them on their flesh. Her breath is brief,
It struggles in the tight cords of her throat . . .
For she is hearing screams above His road.

"We have no king but Caesar."

> *"I know not the Man!"*

"Save Thyself and us if Thou be Christ!"

The stones of Stephen and the wrath of Saul,
The circuses of Nero, catacombs,
The long path winding past the stunted empires,
Fire, the ruined altars, all the lost
And lonely children weeping in the dark,
The gagged mouths, the burned feet, the eyes

Left scorched and empty, dead to any pity,
Martyrs prisoned in the towers, virgins chained,
The persecuted innocent of earth
From Philomena down to the leathered lead
The commissars lift up in smothered rooms . . .
All these are here.

        Yet a green is on the hills,
And dauntless joy is resolute in crags
Thrown strong around them, and behind them on the road.
The meadowed slopes grow gentle to their feet
With yielding, and a screen of trees drops down
To wake a gratitude within them for the fall
Of shadows and the feel of secrecy.

Here is hatred's failure, cruelty's defeat,
The ultimate, humiliating lack
That hides in subtlety.

Egypt! She was glad for Egypt, and the time
It gave to her. These years when she could fold
Her arms for tabernacle, lift her face
To be a sky, and star, and canopy!
And know when she and Joseph poised their hands,
They built Him roof made strong in lonely prayer.

And Joseph's eyes were wider now for quest
Than once they were till Angels came in dreams.
He could not pierce the consequence that God
Place so His cradle in an exile land.

Except that all land be an exile land.

Far back at Bethlehem the Angels wait
And hold in silence voices that will speak
When He has died, when women then will come
To seek Him at a tomb. The voices wait.

11

But Herod-men have marched and prodded straw
With swords and searched a house, and then a stable.

"Women wept; Rachel would not be consoled."

The Herod-men had come and prodded straw.

But voices waited and the word was held.

"He is not here; behold the place where they laid Him."

AND AFTERWARD . . . THEY RETURNED
INTO GALILEE . . . TO NAZARETH

SO easily. . . .
There were no more of dreams,
Nor roads, nor angels counselling of roads
And flight, no more of stars, nor frankincense
And myrrh laid down in tribute as the gold,
Nor more of a Child hugged secretly while eyes
Searched out faint welcome at a stranger's gate.

But only friendly doors at Nazareth,
The afternoons, His quiet table laid
With plate and saucer; stitching of a hem
Drawn through again on threads that moved her hands
In the old way of a woman in her home.

Here Heaven was as casual as leaves
Shawled out to summer. Aeons came to rest.
Who breathed above the void commanding worlds
Be born and space be heavy in the lunge
Of planets, paused, and for these years looked up
To ask permissions and to find her smile.

"He was subject unto them."

                    He took of food
They cupped and gave to Him. He slept and woke
And listened to their footsteps in a room.
He shouted in the air, and ran, and laughed
The singsong syllables habitual
To childhood, telling us we need not fear.

Day dawned with freshened breeze behind it, night
Gloomed and the wicks were bright, a neighbor spoke across

13

A yard where other children played to raise
Sweet rout and echo: cupboards, blankets, beds
And bins, stout raftering; the rain against
A window, wheat and harvest, hunger, sun,
The laundering, all these are Nazareth,
And He was in the midst, was one with us,
Familiar, wearing sandals on a village lane.

His Seraphim were now the nesting birds, His throne,
A stool, His praise, the droning of the bees.
Who cannot change, here grew; Who twirls the earth
Waxed strong, for time became a web above
The Timeless, and at Nazareth, the sum
Of endless, uncreated glory shone
Of faces that He loved.

　　　　　　　　　There is a day to come
When Nazareth will be a place beyond
Her by a journey's length; when strain
Of distant days falls near and He is taut
With choice He must decide for full revealing.
His Father's business stirs above His soul.
It is a day that turns to three days in His loss,
A pain, a shattering, an end of this,
His Nazareth, and end of peace.

　　　　　　　　　　　This day
Shall come, the cottage will be left and He
Stand regal on the Temple porch. But when He feels
Her arms about Him, sees the search sunk deep
In Joseph's eyes, He wills this choice again
For Nazareth, for Nazareth and peace,
His sheltered peace that spreads this little while
To thirty years.

　　　　　　　We could be hesitant,
Omit this Tabor, miss the longer gift

14

He made to her, for Luke and Matthew both
Comply to wisdom of a reticence,
And have no more than meager word to frame
The long sweet years when He was under skies,
And drank at the secret wells of Nazareth.
But He was there. Full ten times all the days
The generations hold of public deed
He granted to a home that was her own.
And when, at last, He stepped beyond her gate
To break the silences, when He was stark
And statured, when His province was the world,
They whispered of Him as they raised the ancient sign . . .
They called Him Nazarene!

        So Joseph knew
The seeding of the parables and saw
Him touch the lilies of a field, heard sheep
And oxen graze beside His path, watched waters
That would feel command and tread, and then
As Joseph listened, he could hear it said to him . . .

The name of Father that shall be a prayer.

But Mary took these days to keep in wonder,
Pondering in heart that she should be
His strength, His needed gift and lengthened love.
And when His moment strikes and all the light
Is gone, when tumult trumpets hate to sound
Above the city's streets, when darkness comes
And He lies naked to the bite of nails. . . .

She may remember that she sewed one day
A garment for Him as she watched Him play,
That Joseph was at ease and near to her
Who felt behind her, crush of waiting trees!

AND THEY SAID: IS NOT THIS
THE CARPENTER'S SON?

THE years then that had hardened on His hands
Had given Him familiar feel of tools.

He shouldered timbers, stooped to brace His back
Beneath the weight of rafters, gripped the rough
And splintered surfaces of boards. The sweat
Stood on His face, His sinews strained and locked
To force the closing of a stubborn joist,
And when He paused to breathe and wipe His brow,
He drank great draughts of water in His thirst.

They saw Him, tall and competent to beams,
A Workman here with others at the place
Of toil, a Carpenter with callouses
And scars upon Him, One Who woke to meet
The day with hunger, stretched beneath the night
In body's want of deep, unbroken sleep.

He was a Man with stride and countenance,
With name, and with a strong voice of His Own.

His speech fell in an accent that they knew,
Of edges, scaffolding, of trestles, nails
And hammers, of decisions and the wood
That must be cut and fitted to a plan:
The full exchange of language in a craft
That gave identity and bond with them.

When Joseph died, His kinsfolk understood:
He would go on to days, and still more days,
In work they recognized, with nothing changed,
Nor more achievement than the daily task
They shared where carpentry on counted boards
Made small construction for a village needs.

17

Yet David, prophet, peering from a past
Had seen the vision of a Workman building
Far beyond this Nazareth: and sang of Him!

Except He build the city, it is vain
And useless labor to repeat a wide
Horizon full of spired, ambitious roofs
That shimmer in the distance like a dream:
Except His be the pattern, houses fall
And cities sink, diminishing, until
They vanish and His ageless tower stands
Alone, not sand-foundationed, but on rock.

All lines of His are sure, His mortise holds
At certainty, and with Him is no pause
Or limit or a height where labor ends.
He lifts and urges upward to Himself:
He builds to permanence.

                    And with Him always,
Testing every structure in the walls,
Co-laborer and partner in the plan,
Is one whose first apprenticeship and will
Gave roof about His Infancy, who watched
Him grow to Manhood in the hardened hands.

She stands here, hidden in a first consent
Beneath His crosstree, finding in her love
Abandoned cornices, rejected beams,
Unmatched and unattended pieces in the strong
Design, the well-hewn shafting, all the length
Of weathered slabs, the posts, the buttresses
He sets to edges in the unresisting fit
And hold against Him. She embraces sums
Of purposes, and with a veil about her head,
Looks upward to the high, unfinished ledge
Where He leans downward to the endless deed.

His speech falls in an accent that they knew,
For full exchange of language in a craft
That gives identity and bond to them.

At Nazareth when Joseph died, they marked
His every plan, for was He not a Carpenter
Who shared the small construction of a village needs?

ANDREW . . . FINDETH FIRST HIS
BROTHER SIMON, AND SAITH
TO HIM . . . WE HAVE FOUND
. . . THE CHRIST

AND now a day falls to the ache of years
That makes an ending for His prefaces,
When tools are tossed to corners and delay
Is done, when reticence no longer holds
Before Him task and limit of a bench,
And He is striding out of Nazareth,
Past door, and home, and border to the swift
Road leading to a river place where time
Has set appointment and a moment waits
To cast the thunder hidden in His name,
Revealing, breaking, cleaving on the earth
The deep division of His ultimate,
Enduring conflict:

            And where John, grown gaunt
With caves and penances, wears camel skin
For vesture of His advent.

            John is thinned
And honed by fasting. He is blade that swings
Against Jerusalem to cut contention,
Freeing long, unwinding centuries
To vast conclusion, he is flame that shades
A desert sun to shadow, scorches rock;
And John is end, is valedictory
For prophet and for promise as his speech
Beats, urgent, with an imminence that cries
To Israel the breaking of a day
Now burst across the present to consume
In final fire all tentative and Templed years.

A Kingdom is at hand! He comes! He comes,
The latchet of Whose shoe no man may kneel
In worthiness to loose!

They watched this John:
They saw him wade the river with his train
Of penitents, and in a strange, new ritual
That was a cleansing, John had given sign!
They winced when admonitions cried again
Of wrath and of the stones that God could raise
To Abraham as children in his seed.

They challenged him to ask if he be Christ,
And heard it bluntly said that he was not,
Nor Moses, nor Elias, for the past
Is done, the axe is laid against the root,
And every tree that offers not a yield
Shall be destroyed and burned beneath the fire.

The calm, white form of Him moved through the crowd
Beneath a canopy of silence while His eyes
Looked straight to John.

                    They made a way for Him
Among them, cleared a path and found their hearts
Were following His slow, unhurried steps
In hush that fell like childhood come again
To be an awe.

            The wind stirred on the waters.
Watching trees were tall and whispering
Across the air.

                He paused, and in His glance
The wide arc of the farthest sky swept near
While He was center to the world that sleeved
About Him as a robe He was assuming,
And would forever wear. Light was on Him now,
Light shone to Him, and then He walked once more
To ripple waters outward at His feet
Until He stood before the face of John

Who wore the leather strappings and the skins
Of beasts, and cried aloud of penances.

The sun wrought crystal prisms in the drops
Above His head, and when His figure bent
In whole obedience and plea, not John,
Nor any man, could read within His eyes.

        *   *   *

Their silence then was more than childhood come
Again to be an awe, for earth was held,
And one brief moment of His full submission forged
The portent of an imminence that was
Already here in future they must share.

High in the air His Paraclete, the Dove,
Had circled, swung with a soaring whiteness clear
Against the blue, to touch upon the leaves
Of murmurous, attendant trees the curve
Of wings that swerved and glided down in small,
Enclosing signatures of grace until
His head had lifted: when the force of Light
Made audible the sounding of His praise:

"Thou art my beloved Son: in thee I am well pleased."

The stretches of the rock and sand beyond
This river place will close about Him soon
To hide Him in His lonely prayer of love
And preparation. He will stare across the night
And watch the faithful torches of the stars
He lighted for this vigil, setting them
At spaces in the dark. He will arise
To glisten in the heat, permitting sun
Be fierce, be merciless on Him Who fused
The sun. He will be hungry. Thirst will swell in Him.

23

Evil will creep near to whisper words!

He will endure such blasphemy; will walk
Defenseless as a Man who might be thrust
By lies, who might be wounded in the old
Assaults outfanged in Eden at the prides
Of men. He will submit to strategy:
But when the lures of Satan have been cast,
He will command: *"Begone!"* to quiver first
Of shudders down the faltered crags of Hell.

"Thou art my beloved Son: in thee I am well pleased."

He will return from stretches of the rock
And sand beyond this river place, and John
Will cry aloud the last, repeated word
That joins Him to the victims that our fathers laid
To Temple altars and which lifts Him far
Above all figures in fulfillment made
Sufficient and supreme. He hears the cry
Of offering, of gift, the single, clear
And utter declaration of His name
That summons liturgies of wood and nails
To send Him on to distant Golgotha.

"Behold the Lamb of God: behold Him who taketh away
the sins of the world."

But now the crystal prisms in the drops
Above His head are falling, and the Dove
Comes Comforter . . . and on His heart in words
And wonder of the conquering consent,
A Voice is sounding an eternal Love.

*   *   *

Amid the throng, a man called Simon stands,
And is unknown except that he is Simon,

24

Here with Andrew, Philip and another John
To be included, and to take such penances
And destiny as fall to fishermen.

Their memories are made of easy shores,
Their expectations trail along mere nets
Of Galilee, and in their thoughts they keep
No more of change or vision, or the speech
Of Pentecost than they embrace the hope
Of dead men come alive, or blinded eyes
That see.

      Till Andrew turns to follow Him
In eager question, and remains to dwell
Beneath His thatch of rushes for the length
Of one day's time. . . .

      When Andrew, running, seeks
His brother, Simon, wrests him from the crowd
And brings him near. . . .

      And they are men who walk
Together on a road with sound of John
Diminishing to echo, past the river's bank,
Past desert, fields, and forward to a town
Where water jars are waiting . . .

      And a wedding feast.

FOR HE WAS TEACHING THEM
AS ONE HAVING AUTHORITY

HERE on His first, eternal mountainside
    The words that had been running like a fire
Across His pathway leap and gather to the high
Commanding flame that is to lift and burn
Forever unextinguished in the dark
Rejections of our world.

                    Here fallacy
Of rank and order in the old appraisal
Is undone, and new nobility is born
To bright distinction. Here is rule, and law,
And judgment made subservient to love.

He speaks now estimate and verdict of His Own.

O you with the calloused hands and doubtful eyes,
O you the unexpectant, you the worried,
You with children tugging at your fears,
You mute, you unpreferred, you unanointed,
You who labor for the daily bread
And stand in no amazement at the hard
Refusals: you the patient, you in homes,
You innocent, you unconsulted, you who wait
Beyond imperial intent or hope
Of deference: O you who crowd among
The shadows and whom courts and chronicles
And crowns account as unresisting shadows,

"You are the light of the world!"

You with the unknown, hidden names, O you
The unregarded, you who bend and lift again
Your strength above fatigues, who know content
An ended day need not be lived again,
Who rise not to the level of esteem
Beyond your children and among your own,

27

"You are the salt of the earth!"

His first, swift journey through the towns is done,
The wine of Cana praised, and they have watched
Him stride abruptly to the Temple porch,
Make whips of cords, tip tables, and unloose
A wrath that cracked like Sinai in their ears.

The questions Nicodemus asked are pressed
Beneath tremendous answers, and the voice of John
Has said, *"He must increase."*

                    A woman at a well
Has brought Him witness: servants running out
Have shouted that a master's son still lives.
Lepers heal, the blind, the cursed, the maimed
Have felt His mercy, even on the Sabbath day.

He is revealed! The Pharisee is spurned!
The power of His name assembles throngs.

But now He stoops here at His teaching place
That is a mountain, and the space around
Him offers tribute as the shadows give
To Light. . . .

                You who have heard it said that less
Than love is adequate, that subterfuge,
Judicious in a prudence, is the law,
That calculation and the public deed
Are full release for hunger in the heart
And terms of destiny, O, all of you
Are children to a Father Who invites
A full bestowal.

             You are children born
Of Him Who makes the suns to rise and rains

To fall on just and on the unjust. You are men,
Are free, and only need to ask to have,
Or knock to find, forgive to be forgiven.

You are seen in secret, followed in the way
Your hearts turn, cherished for the loves you fold,
And all your tragedy is being less than men,
And all defeat is counting costs with God!

For they are blessed who seek not of their own,
But of the Kingdom hold inheritance. . . .
All strategy, and swords, and towered walls
Shall fail; the meek shall win our wearied land. . . .
They are the comforted who feel the tears. . . .
Who hungers after justice, sears his heart
In indignation, finds the bland apologies
Too sweet for savor, scars the night in hot,
Impotent anger, he shall have his fill . . .
And they are wrapped within their own great gift
Returned who give of mercy . . . they are sons
Of God and earn His name who make a peace. . . .
They are the praised who bear the sting of lies . . .
And they who keep the heartsight of a child,
Whose eyes are unconcealed, whose purposes
Are clear as sunlight falling to the crested wave,

"They shall see the face of God!"

And then like flame that is again aflame
With inner essences and deeper veins
That run of fire in fire-consuming dark
For terrible defeat. . . . He cries aloud
His splendor in a freedom for the world.

*"He that doth the will of my Father who is in heaven,
he shall enter into the kingdom of heaven. . . ."*

There was an ending made that day to words
He spoke on the first, eternal mountainside:
He came at last to silence.

                            They would have pled
For more, would hold the night off, slow the day
And pause the very beat within their pulse,
Had such a striving earned them more of words.

But He had ended: and His pathway then
Turned downward on the hill and past their hopes,
Past faces watching, eyes that worshiped Him,
And He was moving onward to a shore
Where boats, and fishermen, and nets await:
To Bethany, to Naim, to Lazarus,
And then to the hill of Tabor where the Light
In full release will give Transfiguration . . .

To Calvary where His words will raise a cross.

AND GOING INTO ONE OF THE SHIPS
THAT WAS SIMON'S HE DESIRED HIM
TO DRAW BACK A LITTLE
FROM THE LAND

THESE were waters Simon Peter knew
As he knew his hand, his doorstep, or the place
His body curved to in release of sleep.
He knew the shallows and the shelves of shore,
The deeps, the eddies, shoals, and where the grey,
Advancing hollows of the waves would slap
Against his slanted keel too heavily for ease,
And whence the sudden winds would brawl to shake
His sails. Genesareth was life to him.

So when the Master, having used the prow
As pulpit, had dismissed the crowd, had turned
To him requesting boats be launched once more,
And nets be cast across the futile surface
That had yielded nothing to their skill,
Simon Peter judged he ought assert
His wiser protest and might offer quick
Dissent in many reasons, patiently.

But then, like one assuming folly to his will,
He had submitted, and the boats had sailed.

Yet now he was not sure, he, Simon Peter,
Seated here with bright accustomed signs
And sounds around him, at his own good helm,
With tug and feel of tiller on his arm,
He, Simon Peter, was not sure.

                    The sky
Enclosed them like a veil, and like the spread
Of dim eternity above them, had no end
And no beginning, and they loomed like forms
Now lost to isolation from a far,
Receded world. There was no time on them,
Nor time around them. They had gone from time
And from the small, confining distances
Of earth with limits and the locking of a shore,

31

And they were freed, and breasted here the surge
Of vast intentions He would choose to tell,
Revealing other seas, and places, names,
Horizons hidden in Himself for share
With them in slow descent of luminous,
Unflickered solitude as held them now.

Then Peter saw his brother and the rest
Intent and waiting, as the waters were,
For sign, or beckon, for a gesture of His hand,
Or word that would release them to His will,
Let time go on again, events resume,
Let sun, and movement, and the winds be freshed,
And let a halted future flow beyond
This stilled, arrested moment to what end
And resolution He had planned. And Simon felt
The love within His eyes surrounding him
In claim and focus as it moved to touch
The others in a warm, inclusive Light,
Forever virtued with a valid potency!

The thought afflicted Simon with his sins,
And a cry, contrite in protest, rose in him,
Nor was it caused by boatsman's reasons or dissent
To sailing, but the fear within himself
Lest tempers sweated in his soul confuse
The wisdom he would need.

                              Until he glanced
To Andrew, sturdy at the mast with listening . . .
And he remembered they had found the Christ,
There at the river place where John had been,
And how a name was changed, and only one,
Not Andrew's, but his own, his . . . Simon Peter's.

Seated here, he was already called
And spoken to in strange and altered accent,

Set apart and summoned to a fate
That seemed to spread and widen in his days
As this enveloping and circled sky
That hung above them . . .

                And he was not sure,
Not sure that all his answers had been made.

The thin, red edge that rimmed Genesareth
Was like the wine of Cana to his sight.
It was glory, like a circled fire, a wound
He had not seen, that somewhere waited him.

"Master, we have labored all the night and have taken
nothing: but at thy word I will let down the net."

And when the ropes had fallen and their hands
Had felt the first, great weighting of the fish,
Simon Peter's heart became a pain
In him. He cried aloud: and then he saw . . .

The Master looking past him to the line of blood
That swung around the world enclosing them.

THE MASTER IS COME AND
CALLETH FOR THEE

AS old as grief this day had waited Him
Since death first cancelled on our earth the use
Of tears and left bewilderment to stare
Against a sodded silence, helplessly.

This is a day imperative to us,
His gift, His difference, and we must search
To find, else incompletion limit Him
And all His words seem but another sun
Of wisdom where our stunned and muffled hearts
Cry out and break against the silence, still
Without an answer.

Here the dirge of trees
That sighs in immemorial threnody
Of whispers over vast assemblies of our dead
Is questioning. . . .

Here furtive winds inclining
Grasses to the unperceptive mounds,
Where futile seasons change and change again,
Are lifted up to touch upon His face
The ache of ancient sorrows. . . .

Here the skies
Are sealed forever in the long enigma
If He turn away.

They who loved
And held His days as treasure, hoarded speech
As wealth, regarded moments of His stay
Beneath their roof as full inheritance,
Had sent their pleading words along a road to Him,
And watched returning roads for swifter love,

But then, in anguish, met defeated end
And emptying, alone: and spiritless
In ritual submissive to the dust,
They walked in slow processional, and sealed a tomb.

As old as grief this day had waited Him
Since death first nullified to earth the use
Of tears and left bewilderment to stare
Against a sodded silence, helplessly.

He had not hastened. He had made delay
Through days, had lingered on the hills to speak
With measured confidence about a sleep
That would be wakened: and when sleep was judged
To be both brief and welcome benefice,
He spoke more plainly: *"Lazarus is dead."*

He had not hastened. He had made delay
And then, in leisure, lingered that the pause
Of time might widen at the darkened gulf
To further distance, that its cleft and sheer
Dividing edge be recognized, while name
And voice and step of Lazarus be lost
To memory, and reference to him
Be fixed inclusion in a patterned past.

And now He stands among their certainties
In kinship with their grief, and on His face
The tears have wetted eloquence to words.

He speaks to Martha in an alms of comforting.

"Thy brother shall rise again."

Martha understood: this time had told
Of other time, and these few days that moved
Along the span of earth's endurance would increase

Above this tomb and know no answering
Until the last. Her tears must wait undried,
Be joined to other tears and they to more
Until the stone be crumbled and the trees
Forget that they were witness in this place
Where death will be forgotten, and the dust
Be only dust to spin anonymous
And unremembered in the winding years.

Her sorrow must go on, repeat its loss
And reach its yearning out like hands that strain
To multiply their pull against the drift
Of far, receding futures . . . when they close
Beneath emerging eras where the skies
Turn unresisting to the long delay.

So giving fee to centuries, she lifts
Old resignation to accepted pain.

*"I know that he shall rise again, in the resurrection at the
last day."*

But He Who twisted cords to make a lash,
Defending in a wrath His Father's house,
Has girded up His heart to take these tears,
Usurping in creation's corridors
His place of peace. His head is bowed. He weeps,
For Martha, Mary, for His Own, for Lazarus;
And then like One Who sees swift, soaring wings,
He calls, commanding, and His Will is noosed
And cast about the years to bring them here
Subservient and nesting in His palm.

He speaks His name and tells identity,
Sets light to flame against the dark, makes wine
Of dust, gives absence food: He spreads His hands
To bid all fears, like little children, cease.

37

"I am the resurrection and the life: he that believeth
in me although he be dead shall live. . . ."

As men who dread what they must swiftly do,
Who turn from horror, tremble at the sight
They must uncover to explore with eyes
And take forever on their souls in scar,
They sweat and labor at a stone. They seek
This Lazarus whom they had shut away!

For He commanded. He had vanquished all
Reluctance, forced them, summoned to His will. . . .

And now the sunlight falls where there should be
No light of sun, and other shadows move
Above the last of shadows wrapped around the cold,
And death stares outward from an opened grave!

He stands here at a margin drawn to time
And set apart to Him, when clay impressed
In earth and mingled with the earth awaits
The purposes that He will breathe again
In image and in likeness of Himself
To make it know, and love, and be a man
With rescued risk and destiny in God!

His voice wakes echo to the farthest sky:

The trees of Eden are remembering.

"Lazarus, come forth!"

The silence then . . . the shivering of awe . . .
This Lazarus, dead Lazarus, had moved!

They watch, transfixed, to see the pulses start.
They shudder at the lift and at the ebb

Of heartbeat, gasp at wrinkles where the bones
Were banded in the ligatures of death. . . .

They watch a hand clutch suddenly at cloth
To tear it from a gaunt and withered throat,
And they will see no more!

                    They cry to Him
For shelter and relief. . . .

                    And then His voice
That thundered in the sky confers a calm
Like light above the sea in infinite,
Enduring sameness on the swing of waves.

    "Loose him, and let him go."

But He Who summoned Lazarus has fled
And sought again a desert place to hide,
For whisperings are running to the gates
Of palaces, and courts are pondering.

He leaves them nothing of an argument.
They hold no counter word to Lazarus:
And all the land is rising at His call.

As deep as grief, this day had waited Him
Since death first nullified to earth the use
Of tears, and after it there is no road
For Him save that which Lazarus had known.

I SAY TO YOU, THAT IF THESE
SHALL HOLD THEIR PEACE,
THE STONES WILL CRY OUT

AND then a peoples' day enarbors Him
When silences are shattered and the poor
Break through to claim their kingdom in a shout!

Worship loses reticence and welcomes Him
In palms and sudden branches of parade.
Their eyes are laughter; living leaves are more
To them than flags. The dust is gold, is gay,
Their caps are crowns, crescendo in their hearts
Cries out . . . for on a road He comes, He comes,
And shawl, and coat, and waving scarves are thrown
Before Him like a canopy pulled down
And cast in tattered tribute to His path.

"Hosanna to the son of David!"

"Blessed is he who cometh in the name of the Lord."

"Hosanna in the Highest!"

In regiments of love they surge to Him:
They turn in ranks and make a formal play
At great procession. They escort: they guard.
They tell His deed and gape at Lazarus.
They pluck the fields and make of stalks their spears.
They throw a cloak to shoulder, sing to Him,
For under trees He comes, He comes, and gives
The deep consent.

He does not hide from them
Forbidding tumult in a word they still
Must heed for loving Him. He comes, He comes
Among them, plain and present to their festivals. . . .

He had petitioned for this ass's colt,
Commanded, mounted, taken retinue,
And then, astride, like Caesar on display,

41

He waved to them, and they could feel His free,
Swift commentary in their hearts. The shouts
Return to hail Him more, and hail again,
Until the city roused and running out,
Asks: "Who is this? What king? What emperor?"

And then as children's song about Him here,
Remembering His years, His parables,
His speech, the high, full statement of His name
In Lazarus, they chant the glad reply.

"This is Jesus, the prophet, from Nazareth of Galilee."

They who had been sibilant in courts
And palaces are lost and buffeted
By crowds they cannot quiet nor persuade
To silence. They are boulders to a tide
Of loves, surrounded, surfed, and overwashed
By exaltation as they lift protesting hands.

"Master, rebuke thy disciples."

But He has ridden past them and His voice
Thrown back across His progress, casually,
Invokes all space and preludes out of time
When worlds yet unestablished waited Him
For origin and purpose in His will.

"If these shall hold their peace, the stones shall cry out."

Like sunlight bursting to the greening wood
Swift welcome to His day investures Him
In Spring with gleam and garmenting of praise.
But brief repeating of the Magi gift
Will soon recede to be for Him a spent,
Forgotten moment of a lost exception.

Even in the midst of it He weeps.

Some turn or merging on the slope of hills,
A vista where the distances are clear,
Has given pause and He has slowed their pace
To look upon Jerusalem with love
That rises in His heart to unheld tears.

O, here the world is, in a hiding place
Of roofs: reluctance, false divisions, steeps
And buttresses of mean refusals: self
Cementing self in self-wrought, rigid walls. . . .

*"If thou hadst known, and that in this thy
day, the things that are to thy peace."*

And when the shouting and hosannas cease,
When whisperings again are audible,
When palms are withered and the dust is laid,
He will return to Bethany and find
Along this road . . . the tatters of a scarf
The hooves have scuffed, the tangle of a shawl.

AND THE WORD WAS MADE FLESH
AND DWELT AMONGST US

WHAT it was that moved beneath this day
Demanding that he find another name
Than time, what end or swift initiate
To longer plan, what deep intensity
Of love now come upon them like a Will
They had not pondered, Peter could not yet
Declare, or whisper to himself in words
When he had sought for answer.

                            They had waked
At Bethany with triumph in their ears,
And would have run again to stand among
The crowding in the Temple, hear Him speak
New parables, to nod their heads in quick
Agreement at their own exalted fates.
They would have smiled, anticipating days
That were to come in endless pageantry . . .
Except that He had paused and did not seek
Jerusalem, nor stride across the dawn,
But closed His eyes as though He strove to hold
A peace that He had known in last of sleep.
He seemed then as a Man Who envied sleep.

They had new need to ask, to beg among
Themselves for counsel, question in a speech
Both blunt and hesitant, what place He chose,
Or if He chose a place, to eat the Pasch?

Then it was, so Simon Peter thought,
The first slim wedge of inference had come.
They asked of Him, and He had looked to them
From far abstracted dreaming, stopped in swift

Attention at the face of Judas, sighed,
And framed a sudden errand, not for Judas,
But for him, for Peter and young John.

These two, He said, must search the city streets
Until they recognize a man with jars
Of water on his shoulder who will guide
Their footsteps to a threshold he will know.

*   *   *

They walked upon the roadway in return
And felt as children who may phrase not words,
Whose eyes tell shining wonder to their world.
For they had found the house, as He had said,
An upper room with table laid, and ranged
Already round it, couches for a feast.
And all their errand was to give a word
The Master would have need for bread, for wine.

The night came, and in Simon Peter's heart
The tapers of a joy were lit more white
Than flared in niches to the Temple roof,
Nor could he speak what lifted him to joy
Unless it be they were alone with Him,
And over them the flood of Paschal moon
Had filled again the mercies of the year.

So step by step, in silence, step by step,
They mounted on a stairway after Him.

Not ever in his life had Peter known
That time could be as waiting as the sea,
Could be as held as waters in the lap
Of noon, could be delayed like sighs or tears,
Yet when he looked again, the Master's hand
Had only circled and had touched the cup
In tender movement to the first of wine.

46

"With desire I have desired to eat this Pasch with you. . . ."

There should not be this sound of murmuring,
Competing voices, straining for a place
At table, pulling at the cloth, this stir
And breaking of a harsh contention, words
Recrossing words, and Peter, quick, insistent,
Turned to add his own impulsive frown.

He looked to find the Master rising up,
And in a silence that was swift rebuke,
In patience that was majesty, in slow,
Unhurried gesture, lay aside His robe,
Divest Himself of tunic, take a cloth
And basin in His hands and kneel like One
Who had become a servant.

                  Peter stared,
Reluctant to believe the visible.
He gasped, and as a child denying pain, he winced,
Then curled to the edge and limit of his couch.

"Lord, thou shalt not wash my feet!"

But now whatever moved beneath this night
Demanding that he find another name
Than time, reached out to scorch him in a new
Confusion, and to burn his heart in fire
He had not thought was consequent to Love,
Or carried in a pledge he once had made.
The Master bowed, and bent to him again.

"If I wash thee not, thou shalt have no part with me."

If such be issue, Peter knew a cry
For whole solution! It was sound in him,
Was like a wave, a tide, a crashing surf

Against the rocks of prudence, and if storm
Be wild within, and over him be dark
Unknowing, still the rescue of consent
To purpose was his own: and in a half
Remembering he heard his voice again.

"Lord, not only my feet, but also my hands and my head."

The level of the shaken world returned
To balance, and the flickering of light
Revealed more seemly shadows as the feast
Subsided to a drone, and Peter looked
To find the Master in His place, while all
The slow traditions of the past began
With nothing changed. These were the forms as old
As memory, and certain as the past
That Peter loved. A wine to tell the gift
Of covenant, the herbs for bitter sign
Of sorrow, bread recalling haste and flight
And long directions through a desert land;
The psalms to be both joy and mourning, songs
For Beauty on the Face that is not seen.

Peter loved such peace, and sighed to mark
The measure of contentment: this was deep
Resumption of a chorused harmony,
An end of discord, blend and weave and fall,
A melody of ease, a promising. . . .

"Amen, amen I say to you, one of you shall betray me."

Had earthquake shattered in the room to leave
Behind a space of disbelief in blank,
Descending horror, Peter would have said
That lesser shudder shivered in his veins
Than he endured. He turned to Philip, thought
He had not heard, yet heard again: *"Amen,
Amen, I say to you that one of you . . ."*

48

This Paschal night? This meeting of the year
With mercy? Here? Among such brethren? Here?
He quivered for remembering his sins,
And took old doubts that he had known for torment.
Here? Betray?

        He sought the face of John
And saw serenity that was a pause
To him and stronger confidence: yet when
The head of John bent forward to a new
Assurance, found the Master's breast in peace,
Then Peter, questioning, had asked a word
And strained to catch the answer, but to find
The Master was attentive then to John,
And afterward to Judas, while the guess
That came to him in whispers only told
That Judas had gone out to seek the poor. . . .
The morrow was a festival . . . the poor . . .

So Simon Peter was released to stroke
And temper in his mind the inner blade
Of his resolving, be a man again,
Be bold before his fears, to scrutinize
The time, and test the strain of what to do
Should enemies appear, and what to say
Should argument be made against his love.

He shut his fingers to a hardened fist,
And gave attention to the Master's voice
That touched now on the very thoughts he met
Within himself, except that Peter caught
A swift, recurring theme he did not wish
Or favor: something of an end, a dark
Finality where none might follow.

"Why cannot I follow thee now? I will lay down my life for
thee."

49

Peter meant his words to be a sound
Of protest, that the time had not dissolved,
That nothing changed, that all was yet as all
Would ever be, and when he cried to deep,
Perplexing regions in himself, and searched
A firm rebuttal, what he seized was still
The shaft of his proposal and the sword
Of good intent already drawn and wielded.
Let everything be said: he now would give. . .

*"Amen, amen, I say to thee, the cock shall not crow, till thou
deny me thrice."*

Beneath him then, the steady earth turned faint
With wavering, the roof where he was housed
Became as air. He spun, and hurtled, reeled
To slanting skies; he put his hand out, clutched
At certainties and saw them crumble, wrung
Away from seeing; shouted to his shame
It was not so, and blindly lurching, found
He could not prove by reassuring feel
Of edges that he stood secure, or saw
Within his summary of self a shield. . . . .

He told himself he had not heard. So soon?
Before the cock-crow? Thrice? While yet this night
Was over him and lighted candles burned?

He looked at John but did not let it seem
He looked. He glanced at Andrew. Philip there,
And Matthew, James. It was not said of them!
Where now had Judas gone? Why had he gone?

Yet there was not a scorn on them, not one.
He noted that. They were not watching him,
And Peter shifted on his couch to move
A little toward the table, took a shred

Of lamb between his fingers. He would eat.
They had not noticed: they were listening.
He turned in painful care to look again,
Then set his own mind so . . . to listening.

The Master had been speaking, and the voice
That Peter loved was like an April sun
Made audible in words to warm the soul
Left lonely in the cold of self resolve.
It was a nourishing to roots that strive
Unaided in a Winter, and must die
Among their own resources. Hope resumed
In Peter while he hungered in his heart
For more than what he was, and yearned for more
Than what he had, or, all alone, could give
In emptying reply: he would be one
With Love that uttered words, and be absorbed
Within the Master as the living flame,
So fused, inseparate, he could not fail
Nor be by distance of his own defeat,
Apart, unfriended and unsanctified.

He felt the warming come to him again.
The Master called them little children here
Who need not fear, nor think themselves alone.

They watched then as the Christ reached out His hand
To gather to Himself the scattered bread
That lay before Him, and a candle's gleam
Ran golden to the chalice when He moved.

He asked for more of wine. His hands were firm
In purposes that touched the bread and filled
The wine-cup deep, as Peter's thought returned
To Cana and the gift of plenitude
That was His way with blind men and the poor
Who cried to Him. Then Peter watched His hands.

They poised above the bread like wings of Will
Before creation, hovered like a grace
Of light across primeval darkness, held
All murmurs through the room in white command
To silence. Peter watched His hands and saw
Them fold like secret strength about a prayer.

His fingers held the bread and with a slow,
Deliberate and ageless motion, broke
To fragments, when His eyes were raised beyond
All vision, past the limits of the stars
Where worlds are incidents and space is frame
About a swift intention that endures
Unhindered to demand of substances,
Submission, and a meek obedience.

He paused, and when a sign embracing them
Had given sweet thanksgiving, Peter's mind
Was racing in the sudden memory
Of other bread, of other fragments saved
And gathered up in baskets on a day
The Master pitied them and multiplied
A dozen crusts to be the fare of thousands.
Peter tasted on his mouth again the crumbs
He had forgotten, and as one so stunned
By revelation he has need for care
And firmer surety, he thought of words
Recalling manna that their fathers ate
And died thereafter: and of living bread
"If any man shall eat, he shall not die."
But Peter's memory was lost beneath
A nearer awe that spread within his heart
When he had looked to see the Master stilled
And waiting in a silence. Then he knew.

"Take ye, and eat. This is my body."

The dish with fragments broken in a Love
Came close and Peter, searching in himself
For sums of adoration he might seize
To set above his sums of sorrow, found
A Name that mutely rose in him for need.

"Thou art the Christ, the Son of the living God."

The candle's gleam that sought the lifted cup
Ran shivering before the whiter gleam
That was His hand again, and Peter felt
Divinity unsatisfied create
New mystery and pour above the dark
Impenetrate of all offenses, gift
And healing that can only come of wounds!

"Drink ye all of this. For this is my blood of the new testament which shall be shed for many unto the remission of sins."

How far away the earth was, or what time
Might seek to make recovery in a year
Of centuries, where breathing might begin
Or pulses start, how he might rise, or move
To recognize his face again, or know
Who Andrew is, or Philip, for the change
In Andrew, in himself, in Philip, all
The rest, were providences Peter left
Unanswered and alone with Him Who was
The Christ and Highpriest, Giver and the Gift,
Who set His words to tremble in the years
Of centuries, and over earth, and names
Of all of them, and over bread and wine.

"Do this for a commemoration of me."

An older day upon the mountainside
Reclaimed the Master, and He spoke again

Sweet cadences of prayer that Peter found
Were still more intimate than they had learned.
He called them friends, not servants, but His friends
Who found in Him identity and Love
That had no more wherewith to give, and when
The fond inclusion in His speech had moved
To Peter like a peace, He spoke of peace
And of the alien counterfeit a world
Might hold and come no nearer to His own
Bestowal than the shadows are to light.

He said they need not wander in a search,
For He is Way; nor gather to compare
Brief answers, He is Truth; nor be astray
In banishment for in them He is Life
And will not fail.

           Peter saw no Dove
Descending in a flurr of wings, nor heard
Compulsions of a voice from Heaven, save
The voice within this rapt and curtained room.
Nowhere on the Master's face was sun
That blinded: yet a cry remembered came
To Peter when his thought returned to Bread
And garments that were shining as the snow.

    "Lord, it is good for us to be here. Let us
    make here tabernacle. Let us stay. . . ."

But when he lifted up his head, the cry
That he had summoned in his need was left
Unuttered as he caught and smothered still
Another cry protesting that an end
Had come to listening, and hopes he had
For making here a dwelling and a home
Be laid before the world's return, be lost
Forever to the tyrannies of time.

The Master stood within a doorway, faced
And open to the night, and John had moved
With Him already through a space so broad
To Peter when he saw, they were as forms
Dissolved by distances he could not span
Nor hold, nor halt by any pleading dreams.

It had been done: the gift had all been made.
Now he had taken, and the Paschal cup
Was dried to last of staining drops that bled
Across the gold. It seemed to Peter then
This room had widened to embrace the earth,
And touched all far horizons at the shores;
These walls had lifted in new gates
And archways as a Temple, and the night
Had grown, expanding till a moon of white
Beneficence became a season set
Without an ending, and that flame and blood
Had reddened in this cup to destinies.

Then Peter knelt and tested in himself
The bond of love. His hand reached to his sword:
He would follow; he would not deny.

LET HIM BE CRUCIFIED!

THE brook of Kedron twisted like a scar
   Of moonlight to their path, and when they crossed
In quick, successive shadows, He had gone
Beyond a destined boundary and reached
His last deserted loneliness of pain.

He came to a Garden waiting in the night,
To trees that were to watch and turn away,
To earth that would be shamed, to time so drawn,
So jagged on His flesh that it would strive
Within itself for swiftness over Him,
To blood that would attempt the use of tears,
To cries that ache for silence, to a chill,
Surrounding darkness that would wish to fold
And warm around Him in defensive love.

He is alone, and henceforth all His pain
And all His burdening must be alone,
For this is night, and this, Gethsemani
Where none may follow, none may move to Him
Companion. He is lost to solace, stripped
Of presence, voice, or any face of friend,
And lonely, takes within the night the edge
Of individual, inventive sin
That separates and cuts to Him like new,
Distinctive evil that had not been slit
Before. He does not dull or grow complacent,
His perception does not wane. He sees,
He feels and touches, but He sees no friend,
Nor feels a sigh, nor reaches to a hand
That He may take in hold of brief relieving.

Only evil, dripped and thickened slime
Of evil, leering, hideous in grin,
In posturing, obscene and cruel, cold
As tyranny and smooth like oil, like flame
To burn, like noise to startle, as a grief

To be deceiving, thumbed and whined and brayed
Around Him, in Him, pressed and bearing down
Above Him, after, bitter in His veins,
Corroding, chafing, vomiting in stench
Abruptly, teasing, laughing in His face
The shrill, staccato blasphemies of Hell!

And all of this in concentrate and sweat
Past measure, long in drain against His heart
That is but One heart, weary and alone.

He could remember her who saw these trees
As far away as childhood, felt this dark
Above Him even on a day most fair
In Nazareth, for she had not been left
To distance by a choosing of her own,
But by an old consent: and would have prayed
And tossed all years of Nazareth aside
For one brief moment in this night with Him.
To speak, be substitute and victim set
Forever in His place! If such could be,
If such indulgence out of Heaven gave
Her happy roads to seek Gethsemani!

But doubts and old rejections cling about
All others: they are cloaks that stretch along
The ground for sleeping. Peter is a dream
And will be less substantial when he wakes.
The voices that had once been raised to Him
Are stilled, the faces of the children, gone,
The Bread forgotten, welcomes put away.
No crowds are turned, competing for His eyes,
Not even hope that won, for lepers, life
And last ingratitude, comes seeking now
Through shadows. Nothing. Not a hand to touch
His garment's hem, no voice to call His name,

But only silence and the whispering
Conspiracies of trees. . . .

                  They shall not be
Pulled down again in triumph to His path;
They are a portent only, lesser trees
That wave and gossip over Him to tell
Of one Tree waiting that shall be His Own
Where He is Fruit so riven to the wood
He hangs in long reversive ripening
From Fruit, blood red and living, to a Fruit,
Death white and cold.

              He shudders and the nails
Are in His mind, the thirst is clutched about
His throat, His breathing is the laboring
Of pain not yet endured, the lash is striped
Across His shoulders, still unmangled, gall
On sponges touches to His lips, the cries,
The heat, the spittle's fall foreknown: the thorns
Are locked in fire, and banded to His head,
Twist tight to agony that will not yield.
He writhes and lifts again to gasp the air
In great repeating sobs, and finds His hands
Are not before Him in a poise of prayer,
Nor does He kneel: His face is wet, and pressed
Against the ground, His arms are wide in grip
And forming of a cross!

            Death, mere death
Itself is kindly, wounds are good, the nails,
Sweet benefice transfixing feet with bliss,
The thorns are easy garlands, every sting
In kiss, denial, lash, is like caress
And multiplying comfort when His soul
Looks inward to accept corruption, sees
Within Himself what fallen form and face

59

He must assume, and on the summit be
Beyond division. He is Adam cast
Again from the ancient garden: He is man
And woman: He is Cain and Sodom, Saul
And Caesar: He is fleshed humanity
In race and tribe and city, in the dark,
Too secret rooms where only Satan smiles,
On continent, and street, and in the dust
That does not now remember that it stood,
Defied, rebelled and spat out sterile prides.

His heart, His lonely man-heart, joyed to brim
With image of His Father, innocent,
Looks down, astonished at its blasphemy!

"Who knew no sin, He hath made sin for us,"

Thought repeats against His thought, the curl
And cunning of perversions. He is red
With murders, foul with lingered usury;
His eyes are darting in the cheapened stealth
And glinting of a fraud. He trembles, bleeds,
He will not look upon Himself! He cries
With pain He should not feel, puts down upon
Himself an inner loathing. He is lost
And stranger; He is tumult, bent, transformed:
A pool where evil sluicing from the drains
Of time is pouring; He is refuge, hut,
Enclosure for the vile. He is alone!
His lips are smirking lips, His fingers, thieves,
His feet that are as blossoms to the earth,
That walk like living springtime, blessing earth,
These feet are lechers' feet!

                And when His soul
Looks upward to His Father, He can see
Not love, but justice and descending wrath.

He hears not now: *"Thou art beloved Son;"*
The sentence falls to Him as one Accursed.

"My Father, if it be possible, let this chalice pass from me!"

The flesh turns fugitive. His pleading mind
Would fly, would run away, compel the soul
And body to refusal, speak the rights
Of guiltlessness, escape, be farthest free.
And then His heart, His lonely man-heart, **heard**
His will, and knew it for the Will of God,
Conformed, and close and wearing bruise for **sign.**

His will takes hold of flesh and soul and mind
And brings them triple victims to His love.

"Nevertheless, not as I will, but as Thou wilt."

Then anguish ceased, and only in the trees
Was whispering and whispering, and soft
Inmingled slantings of the moon. He raised
His head like One returning from afar,
And leaned against a reassuring rock.

He stood then, found His feet could seek, His **hands**
Reach out to shadows; He could move from tree
To tree, and for a moment need not be
Alone, for Peter waited, James and John
And all the others . . . there beyond the dark.

His face, now luminous in need and white
To fingers of the moon, comes searching them;
He pauses for an instant patiently. He turns
Away: and only veils of night receive
In ministry the impress of His drawn,
Discouraged countenance. They are asleep.
Who keep Gethsemani are lost in sleep!

They do not rouse and run to Him, they take
Not dreams and pity in their hands to give
Him comfort, pale and poor assurances
Of love. They ask not: *"Who is this that comes*
From Edom? Why is thy apparel red?
Why thy garments like theirs that tread the winepress?"
Why soil on Him, why tangled hair,
Why sweat that is the remnant of His pain?
They offer no embrace: they are asleep!

He moves within the shadows of the trees
And in His sorrow kneels again to pray.

"Nevertheless, not my will but thine be done."

*   *   *

The line of lanterns swinging in the dark
Traced journeys for an epic soldiery.

They came with staves and ropes and swords, they came
With shield and spear, they came with plans; and first
In strategy, a man named Judas strides.

What think they in their souls, these strategists?
That He will run away, that He will hide?
That He will cower under rocks, place trees
Between Himself and them who urge pursuit?
That He will climb among the caves, elude
Their search, be hare for them, be fugitive?
That He will seek a safety in the tombs
Along this countryside compelling them
To cunning, quick resolve in bold campaign?

Peter, James and John, the others wake
To find no marks upon Him of the deep
Enduring that they had not shared, no scars

Of conflict, nothing of a change, no sign
That He had writhed while still they slept, had begged
For pity. He is tall and sure, and now
Among them looks to lanterns swinging near.

They were rejoiced, for out of darkness then
A voice they cherished called, a form they knew
Discarded shadows. Judas had returned.
He had embraced the Master. Judas swung
Wide arms around Him, kissed and clung to Him.
They were made glad, for Judas had returned.

Until they heard the tolling of a love.

"Judas, dost thou betray the Son of Man with a kiss?"

For space of heartbreak there is pause on Him.
Then silence lay like a limp and fallen shroud.

He stared beyond the lanterns to the press
Of faceless figures circled in the dark:
Here in the dimness He is tall and sure
And when the torches lift, discerning Him,
He gives them back a question like a gong.

"Whom seek ye?"

The thin indictment answers Him, His name.

"Jesus of Nazareth."

Peter, James and John, the rest who keep
With Him this little while, remember slopes
That were His first eternal mountainside,
And listen to the accent He had raised
Instructing other shadows they are Light.
They hear again the sound in Him that filled

Their nets, that uttered to the Bread command,
That spoke to death and out of Lazarus
Compelled reply of movement in a tomb . . .
For He gives challenge, makes profession, throws
His summons to the night in single cast
Of all our prophecies to all our years.

"I am He!"

The soldiery and faces make retreat,
The torches waver, scuffling and the scrape
Of sandals mar the purpose of advance,
And one of them has fallen in a wound
That Peter's sword, bright flashing to the moon,
Has cut to prove that sleep no longer holds
Nor dulls in him the pledges he had made.

*"Put up again thy sword into its place . . . thinkest thou
that I cannot ask my Father and he will give me presently
more than twelve legions of angels. . . ."*

Their confidence renews in circles closed
About Him, torches lift in victory,
And walls of shoulders unafraid press tight
Around Him. He is caught. They shout the news
In taunts and cries defying angels, winds
And shadows, any trees or other friends
Defensive that are near, and when they cease
And separate, stand panting to the moon
In battle boldly won, when they re-form
To squadrons, He is there . . . alone.

His hands
Are roped and He is tethered to their will.
They pull and He must move to them, they pull
For jest, and He must halt. They laugh. Alone.
His feet are helpless: they may bare His feet,
Unsandal Him, may force His steps to thorns

If they demand. Their malice is content,
With nothing more to fear or plan or do.

The space of waiting time, the trees, the winds,
The shadows of Gethsemani are free.

*   *   *

Caiaphas is fringe and a robe of gold
That stiffens in embroidery to ask
Old questions he had woven in his mind
As devious as patterns, and like threads
Intended to achieve a certain show
And shimmer of magnificence. He speaks
In complicated forms, and sets the theme
Of first inquiry on the patient plane
Of general and cultivated search
For issues: there had been some theories,
Perhaps, some notions of an ethic shape
More personal and private than are met
In common law? Some speeches had been made,
Some sermons, even, that might well impress
The gullible? Just what report, what sum
And survey could the Culprit give to clear
These matters for His judges who, indeed,
Regard traditions and the curbs of love
A sore responsibility?

The whine
Of wearied language spins beneath a night
Long drawn from innocence of day, and lamps
Hang fire around Him of a vigil kept
Apart from morning. He can look to find
Quick secrets in their eyes, and antecedent
Verdict made already plain. His hands
That had not preached are bound, and at His side
Rebuttals take the shapes of clubs and swords.

65

"In secret I have spoken nothing. Why asketh thou me? Ask them who have heard."

> The fist against His face was like a shock
> Of unbelievable and thrusted fact
> That suddenly was true. He had been struck!
> The sting, the flash of light, the hurt were real.
> He tasted blood upon His lips, felt tears
> Within His eyes. He swallowed, tried to breathe,
> And hands, involuntary, sought to touch
> His cheek.

> Not pain, not anguish in Him now,
> But ignominy and the salt of shame.
> A man had turned, invading, formed a fist
> To mall, insult, and soil His human face!

> He staggered once, and then a calm returned
> To put a lonely quiet on His voice.

"If I have spoken evil, show where is the evil: but if well, why strikest thou me?"

> So Caiaphas in golden garments knew
> Remaining night must dwindle to a search
> For witnesses, for others in the mould
> And mood of Judas. Where was Judas now?
> With languid fingers Caiaphas had made
> Dismissal, stood, but did not wonder more
> What further humors might descend to Him
> Who bore, already, blood upon His face.

> They clattered at the cobbles in a brief,
> Undisciplined and eager march to cells
> Where doors are barred, and soldiers keep a time
> With captives. He is pulled and hurried past
> An interval of sweet relieving air,

66

And when He stumbles, turns His eyes and looks
Across the courtyard to a fitful flame,
He sees, in swift and darkened silhouette,
The form of Peter with an arm upraised
In heavy gesture to a serving maid.

And then a door is locked, and He is shut
To other arms and hands and other forms
Surrounding Him. They shuffle near, they hood
His head with cloth, they strike, they strike again
To ask: "Who struck thee? Make more prophecy,
Which stick, which rod?" And then they snatch the cloth,
And He is dizzied in the whirling maze
Until He falls:

                    To keep for comforting
The glimpse He had of Peter in the night.

At dawn the formal fringes swung again,
And unto Caiaphas came more and more
Of crusted garments met and multiplied
Like shows and tiers and terraces of law
Where far beneath them, roped and bruised and torn,
The Prisoner is shining in the glow
Reflected of their daylight purposes.

He stands, and He is silent while they move
Their heads in unison to watch the creep
And entrance of the witnesses, and wait
In calculated pause for hearing words.
They break then, glitter to a quick confusion.
Words are shattered, evidences chip
Before them in the splinter and the crack
Of contradiction. Witnesses retreat.

So Caiaphas has risen like a proud,
Commanding tower in their midst to lift

Prestige above their heads and give them glow
Of honor in the questions he will pose:
Yet when he speaks, they frown, for they have heard
No answer, when he speaks again, they smile
For he has touched upon the very tip
And edge of their intent, and when he puts
His last and solemn summons to the test
Of oath, they lean, expectant, for the weight
And crush of all accusing has been made.

*"I adjure thee, by the living God, that thou tell
us if thou be the Christ, the Son of God."*

Now speech of Daniel to the ancient years
Leaps bright from long delay, and prophecies
Are rescued to a living utterance:
Sweet David sings and reaches from the past,
To teach this moment His eternal song.

His hands, still bound, are lifted, and His voice
Breaks through the silence. He accepts this Name:
He looks to little fringes, He is tall,
And under Him the planets are, and stars.

"I am."

*"And you shall see the Son of Man sitting on the right hand
of the power of God, and coming with the clouds of heaven."*

The shout that answers is a hope unloosed
To triumph swelling of its own increase
And tumult until hate becomes the will
To hate, and will becomes the need, like lust
Engendering a greater lust so lost
Of limit it demands devoured worlds.
They rage at Him, they cry: "No more, no more
Of witnesses," and Caiaphas has ripped

His robe to hold the tattered shreds in flags
Of death. He is condemned. They shout again:
"He's not the Christ, He's not, He's not the Christ,
He's doomed and damned and guilty of a dream."
And then like foam that for a moment clings
And glides before the breaking of a wave,
They come together for the final cast
Of balloting. His judgment is complete.

They are as tides of hatred now unrolled
And deepened, and they move beneath the sky
In dark, unheld, relentless floods of will,
That mount and move to end and purposing.
They tumble to the streets, assemble crowds,
They shout, they call His Name, His crime, and fling
Their voices to the rooftops bringing down
Recruits to swell their numbers, more of heads
For counting, legs to tread with them the dust
Of roadway to the Roman governor,
More hands to spread in protest, more of men
And women, husbands, wives, more poor, more lame,
More halt, for He, Seducer, in their midst
Is judged, and like a lost, abandoned foe
Who once was too elusive, He is caught. . . .

Pilate in his doorway feels the tide
And turns to meet it with imperial
And cool contempt. He toys above the flood
With questions, turns, and turns again to touch
Upon philosophy, to ask of Truth
If truth, indeed, can be, while glints of small,
Unseeking laughter light his eyes. But tides
Are strong around him making politic
And caesared seeps against his hidden fears.

They draw and pull and mount till Pilate looks
Again upon this Man Who is a King,

And ponders whether kingdoms, even those
Beyond the world, are alternates to Rome?

In burst of prudence he has breasted tides
And sends them rushing, rolling in the street
To Herod. Herod is a king and keeps
In Galilee a scepter of a sort.
Let Herod rule, let Herod take the gain
Or consequence of verdict, let him be
Escape for Pilate, earned in sophistry.

But Pilate's smile is where his smile began.
They are returned. They lap and swell and surge
About his hallways in a tumult spread
Beyond the limits of his court. They crowd
Against the stairs, to spill in overflow
And beat against reluctance held to them,
And in the midst, like innocence new gowned,
He stands: and the robe that Herod gave to Him
Is the white, intended garment of a fool.

In His heart, His lonely man-heart, then
Some pulse of gratitude for Pilate paused
The long, accumulating weight of pain?
He sees a hand upraised and hears a speech
Protesting in defense, and if the choice
And preference are soon to change before
The fear of Caesar, if the hand is soon
To fail and seek the cleansing of a dish,
Yet Pilate, for a moment, raised a hand,
And for a moment spoke of guiltlessness!

The whirl and fury of a last exchange,
The words debating Him, the counter words,
The fists uplifted and the fists flung down,
The threats, the arguments are cast like nets
About Him, closing in a plan that draws
To tight conclusion.

Then He hears a name
Announced and coupled with His Own for choice,
And over Him the dark hosannas rise
That give Barabbas freedom to their loves.

There is no margin more, no halt, no last
Retarding of a moment born with Him,
For Pilate, high above Him on a peak
Of lost creation, Pilate looking down
Has asked a question, and the long reply
Has bayed against the marbles, struck the stones,
Reechoed to the hills, astonished skies,
Has shaken space and trembled to the edge
Of stars, and then returns to break within
His held and offered heart that is alone.

"What shall I do with Jesus that is called the Christ?"

"Let Him be crucified!"

The pillar is a sudden blindness thrust
Against His face, and makes a span of stone
Horizons for His eyes. His brow, His cheeks
Are bruised against the stone, His hands are latched
Above Him; He is stripped and stretched, His flesh
Is naked to their stroke, and then the scream
And cutting of the first of whips destroys
A world and all horizons as He writhes
And quivers to another world that crosses,
Curls, and forks along His back in burn
And bite of spiral in the coils of pain
Enmeshed around Him like a latticing
And cage. They turned Him, twisted Him, they curved
Him to a fresh submission, and He soaked
New rains of lashes, falling, falling, falling,
Till He found they had unlinked His arms
And whips were stilled.

71

                    This was the earth beneath
His body, earth that need not now be dreamed,
Nor feared, nor prayed against, for He was sprawled
And broken on the earth, and could uplift
His head to look across a sodden place
That was forever past Him, wet, and sealed!

He leaned against the pillar's butt and breathed
A long, sweet moment that was grateful ease
If only for the cease of falling fire,
And nothing more to be endured or won,
Or satisfied before the love He wore
In wounds could bleed again to be the robe
And regal garment of His further love.

His hand had touched His face, and cleared His eyes
To visions of the soldiers' boots that moved
To Him. He gasped and made attempt to rise,
Obedient, but faltered, failed and felt
His body gripped and dragged astride a stool
While in His heart He heard the laughter fall
In soft renewal of the lash.

                    A palm
Had struck His face. They propped Him, made Him sit
In attitudes, assume a stiffer pose,
Be king for them, hold semblance of a court.
A cloak was draped about Him, and a reed
Stood scepter in His hand. He watched them kneel
Subservient. He saw them come to Him
In smirk and mincing curtsy, felt their touch
Upon His brow, their measuring, and when
The pain, like rings and pointed streaks of blind,
Exploded light had dulled to let Him see,
When tears were ended, and His blood had gone
Past first bestowal to the thorns, His head

Uplifted in a sign of majesty
That willed this newer Love, and wore its crown!

The stairs before Him were a multitude
Of cliffs to be achieved, and one by one,
Exacted slow imprint of feet, until
He gained to levels of a judgment place
And found that Pilate in a long debate
Was sure the balance of a destiny
Remained in spoken words. He heard a cry
From Pilate, felt a bleeding in His wounds,
Met faces seeking Him, and then in crown,
In robe, with scepter in His hand, with scar
And signature of lash across His flesh,
He knew He was exhibited and set
Upon a ledge for pitying.

                    His heart,
His lonely man-heart, then abandoned skies,
And pain, and thorns, abandoned Pilate, left
Their shouting to a silence, reached beyond
This roof, this chill confining cave of time,
And closed upon eternity to hold
It small: and when His heart was warmed, He spoke
The last brief words that Pilate is to hear.

   "Thou shouldst not have any power against me
   unless it were given thee from above. . . ."

His feet descend the stairs, and one by one,
He stains them in impress of feet that now
Will not return. A pathway has begun.
He moves, He treads upon His road of blood
And knows directions, and He will not pause,
Nor fail, nor seek exempting. He has walked
His first few paces; He will not delay.
The pillar is a past, and Pilate's tryst

With bargaining is on Him for a crown.
"Lift up ye gates and be ye lifted up"
For He is moving, marching to the hill
And promise that has waited Him since dark
Had opened and a midnight made a dawn.

We stare at Him. We separate a long,
Expectant lane that closes after Him
In thick crowds crying to the street, and then,
Above us, like a frame of manhood cut
In Hell to imitate a Man, like form
And mockery of limbs, like Bethlehem
Reduced to wood, like blasphemy in arms
That may not fold and feet that may not walk,
In faceless, eyeless, speechless parody,
He sees the Cross that He must clothe with life,
And cover with His flesh that It might bleed!

He feels It there, above Him, drawn and set
Against the innocent and helpless sky.
In tracing of the black geometry
That plans all chaos, save that He is here
To stretch It on Himself and give It love
For center and design. And then the beams
That were as wings of evil on the air
Swoop down and in the nesting of His first
Embrace, become His mercy. He is bowed
And bent, and on His shoulder wood has dug
Its wound; He falters, and His eyes are blind;
He staggers, but He does not fall. It moves.

The sudden lifting of Its weight was swift
In giddy freedom, and His step had lurched
Far forward aimlessly. He put His hand
Before Him, stopped and stumbled, waited blows,
Made measure of Himself in time and pain

That might reveal a task already done
And Golgotha a hill that was achieved.

To find the same sky over Him, and roads
Diminished only by the width of stones.

Who walked upon the waters, saw His path
Heave out before Him like a swollen sea
That still must be subdued, and step by step,
Must be unstormed and brought into a calm
For destined feet. He reaches for His Cross
Again but meets the crackle of a curse
To cast Him forward: then His heart repeats
In pulses of His blood another sound
That He can hear. A man behind Him takes
His cross. He hears new footsteps following!

The women were assembled tears to reach
Him pity, and they cry to Him a grief
For wounds. He speaks to them, and if in voice
He soothes and gives a comfort, in His words
An iron wisdom stands that they must learn
To weep with deeper honor for themselves
And for their children. Then He moves away.

He drags on past a corner, past a gate.
His shadow in the sun is not a Man
But is an angled brace of carpentry
That totters, towers, gains a rescued inch
For balance, wavers higher, and is cracked
And crashed like rubble to the rising dust
Of ruin.

        They are close around Him now;
They circle, watch Him, estimate the twitch
And tremor in His legs, and then they lean
To strain as laborers at stubborn beams

Releasing Him. The dust cakes in His mouth. . . .
He would lie here on the earth to sleep,
Forever . . . while the shrill, defeated cries
Above Him fade and faint away, and swim
To sinking silences. His arms push strong
Against the earth, His face is free, His knees
Drag slow and sweated furrows in their crawl
Until His back and knuckles make an arc
And He is Will, submission, and a form
Bent down consenting to demanded Love.

He lifts His head, and in a moment rimmed
In prophecy and closing all our years
Since Adam, takes His cross again and strains
Beneath It to the crests of Golgotha.

Unbidden winds of April curl to Him,
And weaving fragrance to the airs of Spring,
Are delicate in vesture of a young,
More luminous adorning, that is His
When a seamless robe has fallen to the ground,
And He is naked to the burn of nails.

Horizons ancient in the grip of hills
Tipped up like empty saucers to His eyes,
And when their swinging ceased and all the sky
Held steady in a dome of blue, He felt
Against His back the stretch of wood laid flat
And long beneath Him. He is pressed and pulled;
He stiffens to a line; His arm is seized
And twisted; then a sky that had been whole
Splits red and rips apart in spurt of black
Down screaming lightning centered in His hand!

He is alive with pain: His body lifts
And turns and quivers as the lightning streaks
Again, and iron thunder cracks and breaks

76

And shatters in the dark beneath His blood
Until the tremors in His flesh are stopped,
And breathing, He discovers He is vised.
His body forms a frame to hold a frame;
He is a Man made one with blunted beams!

Then slant of sky slides slowly to the edge
Of distance, and the sinking earth recedes
And falls away until the level disk
Lies dark beneath Him, and His eyes are fixed
Upon the circles of the world! He hangs
At center, feels the deep and steady drag
Against the nails, and when His body's weight
Is endless pull of pain within His hands,
His feet press downward, and He writhes again.

His head is swinging, and the earth is wheeled
With reeling in a spin beneath Him; rims
Of mountains shiver to the whirl of hills,
And He is leaning to the flattened roofs
That climb and mount and pile across the sun
Like loosened sepulchres that had been walls
To vast Jerusalem. And then the light
Is bronze against Him in a sheet of stilled,
Unblinking time that does not stir, nor yield,
Nor turn aside, nor cease, nor cover pain.

Their voices rise to Him from distant pits.
They are like echoes of an ended world
He once had known where men with hands and feet
Could move among contentions and be brave
With gesture. He could hear them, feel their stride
And strut along the ground, receive their scorn,
Their laughter, know that they were tall and bold
And beckoning to Him that He come down,
Come down and be a Man again in whole,

Unfastened body that will need a robe
And pathway to the pardons of the world.

"Father, forgive them, for they know not what they do."

The blood swelled sickly in His mouth, and breath
Was ended, and His heart was all He heard.

Somewhere, as a bird might sing to Him,
Above Him, level to His hair, so near
He need not search, nor move, nor seek for space
Of quiet in the sounding of His blood,
He hears a voice that begs last royal gift
Of brief remembering. He cannot see,
And wrenching now athwart the rigid wood,
His head uplifted, pulling at the nails,
He cannot reach least moment of relief
That He may bring to eyes that seek His Own.
They are two faces in the sun, so fixed
Against the posts they must stare outward only,
Separate, and must declare their loves
In quick companionship of lonely words.

"This day thou shalt be with me in Paradise."

The light is bronze against Him in a sheet
Of stilled, unblinking time that does not move,
Nor yield, nor cease until a shimmering
Like golden curtains comes, and looking down,
He finds that time has folded to a long,
Bright, gleaming coronal, and she is there.

He does not look away, He watches her,
And the light that was a crown about her, breaks,
Increases, brightens, and becomes a path
Where she is mounting, mounting up to Him,
Not for comfort, nor for any kiss

Of soothing, not to lessen Him nor ask
His hands refuse these nails for Infancy:
Not to soften, not unloose the years!
He seeks her here and in her heart He finds
Too deep a silence for the need of tears,
For new Announcement bleeds in her, so old
It is Gethsemani, and Nazareth,
Fused and sealed within a single will
That still is crying: *"This be done to me."*

"Woman, behold thy Son."

The dark was like a thin, descending shroud
Of cold that closed around the world and left
Him shivering beneath an ashen sun.

The wind was chill upon Him, stirred His hair
In faint and lonely movement, and the dust
That lay along the barren rocks had raised
And sifted softly when the wind had gone.
He was alone: and in His hands the nails
Were cinders of a fire that once had flamed
And reddened in His blood, but now had dulled
To crusting of a spread, accustomed pain,
Without a plan.

        He wearied of His crown;
His head that had been bowed upon His breast
Tossed upward in a search for any friend,
To find around Him blackness and the deep,
Unstarred abysses where creation's Word
Has hung no light or mercy to the blank
Rejections of a worse than primal dark.

The wind that knifed across His shivered soul
Came cutting from the frozen lids of Hell. . . .

"My God, my God, why hast Thou forsaken me?"

Thereafter, time on Him became a slow,
Eventless draining and His body sagged
And ebbed and whitened in the drip of long,
Increasing silences that breathed and soaked
And mingled on His limbs until the flow
Pulled down from Him all semblance to a Man,
To make Him but a Wound that hung from nails.

He does not move nor murmur to the dark,
And now is gone beyond His search or hope
For friends who might, in grieving, come to Him;
His eyes lie closed, but when His hand had strained
Against the stake, and helpless, tried to brush
The dried and stiffened cavern of His mouth,
He whispered, and they heard His human need.

"I thirst."

A sponge upon a reed was thrust to Him,
And He Who gave good wine had tasted sharp,
Astringent vinegars that were the last
Of favors that our earth could give to Him.

He wakened; He was tall again and taut
Against the throning of His cross; His head
Was crowned, and on Him majesty returned.
He drank the air and as a Man who sees
Far kingdoms over continents beyond
The sun, He traces with His eyes the dim,
Receding circles of the world. He feels
The freedom of His hands, the swing, the lope
And striding of His feet; He feels His heart
Within Him beating to the endless stroke
Of Infinite, and swelling to subdue
The vast dimensions of forgotten time.

He stands, He towers, He is Adam come
Again to the ancient garden: He is man
And woman, He is Paul and Magdalen,
The martyrs, housewives, sinners and the saints.

And then His love is falling on the hills,
The roads, the little sea that had been dear.
He touches to the mountain where He spoke
His prayer, and He remembers Bread. His hands
Enclose again the smiling of a child.
They test the tumult of the fish in nets.
He hears the echoed word He said to John
And Martha: Peter keeps command against
The years. The cot and table that He knew
At Nazareth are not afar from Him.
And He remembers Joseph and the straw.

Then breath is great within Him. He is tall
And upward from His cross, His voice ascends
To break confining spaces of the stars
And thrusts His triumph past the end of stars.

"It is finished!"

His head is sinking: peace is on His brow.

"Father, into Thy hands I commend my spirit."

This sterile wood He carried to the hill
Has burgeoned with His meaning, and the Tree
Of good and evil, standing in all storm
And contradiction, waits the endless Spring.

WOMAN, WHY WEEPEST THOU?

THE dreams that hovered on the fitful sleep
Of two nights' tears could not be shut away
Nor ended as the dark was ending now,
And when they waked and clustered in the fogs
Of morning, they were women who could raise
Above their loves no speech of Him save hoarse
And stricken whisperings: for they had felt
The death-cold on His limbs, had seen His eyes
That drilled the sky in fixed, unmoving rods
Of hollow stare. They had been witnesses
To holes within His feet, had traced His scars,
The furrow where a spear had dug His heart,
The purple welting of the whips, and when
They turned away, they carried to their cots
The sight of thorns dry-crusted in His blood
As she had lifted them, and in a long,
Maternal hope, arranged again His hair.

They moved around Him: He was soiled, and drained
And heavy to their hands as they had washed
His body and had pressed against His side
The last confessions Nicodemus brought
In myrrh, and aloes, and sweet-smelling balm.
And they had watched and counted in new loss
The bands of linen that were winding, winding
On His form until the last cloth closed
Away His face and He was left a white,
Unyielding burden on the ground for brief
And managed passage to an alien grave.

But now the Sabbath and the dark were done,
And small, relieving tasks their loves had planned

Awaited them. They spoke aloud His name,
Gave quick exchange of empty comforting,
And then their whispers ceased, and they were grey,
Unsandaled pilgrims bending in a shawled
Procession to the dawn.

                              And one of them
Could find no reasons why there should be dawn,
Or day, or night, or longer drag to time
Impoverished of purposes, or hope,
Or semblance of an aim. She had no more
Of tears to shed, nor more of anything.
The earth had ended, all the hills were pose
And boasting, they were shadows only cast
At lesser shadows; trees were false, and fields
Were withered in the lie that summer suns
Could make them green; the winds were wanderers
Uncompassed to confusion where had once
Been steady sky; and every road and path
Her steps might take were but a wandering
With no direction more than any road
Or path that led to nowhere. He was dead!
Who spoke and made her Magdalen was dead!

Out there a tomb was looming like a globe
Of cold, and He was sheeted in the cold;
Upon His feet the linens made a shroud
Against her seeking ministry of hair,
And love, and ointment broken in the box
Of full bequeathing. He had died! The voice
That called and quickened her to life was stilled.
His eyes were lidded, He had vanished past
Her need forever, and her search might beg
Across the wisdoms of a thousand years,
Be heard and smothered in the useless fall
Of all assurances, and still not find

His peace. For He was peace, and in a world
Without Him, there could be no other peace.

Yet she was here, was walking in the mists
Obedient to leading; followed ghosts
Of women over skulled and barren hills,
And when they paused to counsel with themselves
About a stone that had been rolled against
His tomb, then Magdalen could weep afresh
And know the answers in His eyes to tears
Had died, as He had died, and prayers had burned
Away like flames beneath a final dark.

Yet she was here . . . and this was after Him.
He had been. She had found Him, touched the edge
And trailing of His garment when His words
Became her breath. But He was gone. And now
No more of words, for this was after Him.

They moved beneath the hill that raised His cross,
And shivered in the valley of a deep,
Enclosing absence while the sounds of haste
Above their steps were fears and memories
That hurried them to seek a farther ridge
Beyond this place, and where the morning gleamed
In slant of kinder sun. She followed them,
And save that in her love she would not pass,
Nor ever leave, nor look beyond this hill,
She had consented to their fears, and as
They halted, gathered on the rim of light
To call to her, she was not far away.

She saw them. They were pointing with their hands.
They stood and gestured in the light and wept
The name of Him Who died. She saw them there.
Then tremor on their voices reached to her
Who now was suddenly alive to blades

Of flashed and whetted meaning. They were held,
Transfixed upon their path by newer fears!
Some harm, some swift event. . . .

                      And Magdalen
Had clutched their shaken shoulders and with head
Upthrusted sought for visions in the sun
Of darker evil that might be her own
To strike and vanquish. She had challenged worlds,
And aeons, demons out of Hell, until
Like alabaster shining in the light
Of centered morning, like a rounded roof
Of silence undefended to the day,
She saw His tomb: and took upon her heart
The wound of open doorway where a stone
Should still be sealed!

                 Her feet against the earth
Were pale, repeating pleas that space be brief
And winds be on her hair for eagle flight
To Peter's threshold and the house where John
Lay sleeping. She was envious of air
Or thunder that could break above the hills
Unfettered and be instant in the burst
Of sound. She wanted wings, and speed, and cries
To run ahead like waves; she longed for hands
To pull horizons down to cast them smooth
Beneath her scorning heels, that over walls
Of wide Jerusalem be swifter roads.

Then streets set barriers to her and gates
Were goads, the markets were a throng of thick
Impossibles retarding haste; the turns
And paving to a distant door were pain
Of anguish till an end was made and fists
Tight curled had raised like living clubs to beat
On Peter's casement at the house where John

Lay still asleep. And when they roused and stood
Above her, Magdalen, stretched flat to earth,
Could lift no other language than a sob.

His body was molested! He was touched,
Invaded, even death was not enough
For peace; the hate that nailed Him to a cross
Had split His tomb and levered at the stone
Left guardian! The stone was rolled away,
Was not in place; His body had been harmed. . . .

She wept alone, and seeking in her tears
For comfort, knew that Peter and young John
Had not awaited more of broken sobs,
But fled to be themselves a living stone,
A guard, and seal, if need be, at His tomb.
And Magdalen could wonder in her heart
If Peter wore his sword.

               Peter knew.
He knew forgiveness: he was one who held
Within his soul the secrets of himself
And shared in deeper meanings of her tears.
Peter knew. And John, young John, beloved
Among them all, who bore an innocence
As gift and measure of his love, young John
Would run on swifter roads than she had found. . . .

        *   *   *

The long, returning path was slower time
And darker than her grief had yet endured
Or thought was possible. She could not turn,
Nor move, nor kneel to scan the lonely sky
Asserting even in His death that He
Was there, concealed beneath a place she knew
And still could think of as direction drawn

Across her heart for vigils. He was lost
To her, as she was lost; and when her eyes
Discovered Golgotha again, a deep
Perceiving gratitude arose in her
That need, unguided and alone, had brought
Her here, and that her wandering was wise.

She looked upon the hill that yet preserved
The last great sounding of His voice. Unseen,
She saw Him on the Tree where He had hung
To grant the sweet forgiveness she had found,
To soldiers who had known Him not. She heard
The echoed accent of His speech until
Her grief, unable for a longer pain,
Sought company of things: and she was swift
In mounting past the ridge again, to run
Through gardens where His own had carried Him,
To stones where He had lain, to twigs and trunks
Of other trees that stood as sentinels
Above His tomb. She yet would touch the stone,
Pour warm profusion to its empty chill,
Be near, be near. . . .

                   His tomb was like a last,
Abandoned fortress made untenable,
And rose before her like a battle lost.
She stooped to peer across the opened door
To cry to dark its false security.
But forms angelical were there in robes
Of Light rebuking all submission to the dark.

"Woman, why weepest thou?"

"They have taken away my Lord; and I know not where they have laid him."

They who seemed so confident of Light
Gave no reply, and she could mourn again

And turn to find her search upon the vast,
Outspreading earth begins in gardens, here,
Where trees are striving for the touch of Spring,
In this bright place where gardeners might be. . . .

She hears behind her snapping of a twig,
And then a footfall come upon the ground.

"Woman, why weepest thou?"

She would enforce an answer, make demand,
Bring end, conclusion, she would know!
So she was shouting to the kindred trees,

*"Sir, if thou hast taken him hence, tell me where thou hast
laid him."*

The space then in the pulse of beating time
Was as her heart in wait of love, for Love.

"Mary!"

The sounding of His voice created worlds,
And through the cold, unlighted distances
Of void beneath her, reached to bid her live,
Inhabit, breathe and be candescent heart
Of endless penitence! She held great gifts
Of newer pardon, for His uttered word
Absolved her of the sackcloth of His death
And set her free. She is a soul reborn,
Possessed of Heavens, nascent in a peace
She thought forever shattered and denied.

"Rabboni!"

The sum of hope in living is this word
She speaks now to the Living in a love

That has no higher Word. She does not ask
Or question, seeks not for the bitter wounds;
She hears a name and knows it for her own,
And pleads no more than that His voice pronounce
Her name: and then her eyes, adoring Him,
Are ecstasies that He is He, and near!

She watches movement on His face and finds
The wind against His garment is a new,
An unexpected prayer that she might try,
That shadows of the trees are light to Him,
That when His fingers lift beneath the sun
They make more shadows, and that all of Him,
His voice, His countenance, His opened eyes,
All these are gifts that Magi bring to Him!

Her trembling hands are silences of prayer,
And slowly reach to touch His living feet.

*"Do not touch me . . . but go to my brethren and say
to them . . . I ascend to my Father and your Father."*

And when He ceases, and she sees no more
The risen wonder of His face, when voice
Is ended and He stands no longer near,
Complying softly in obedience,
She goes to Peter's sorrows, and young John's.

YE MEN OF GALILEE, WHY STAND
YOU LOOKING UP . . . ?

THE dawn, thereafter, was a day that blared
Above them in a trumpeting of sun
And would not fade, nor soften in its fierce,
Announcing triumph till they heard, and all
Jerusalem had heard, and skies had caught
The echo that will be within the light
Of every breaking morning till the last.

Caiaphas has shut his ears and sworn
Abroad his perjury that Roman guards
In sleep had failed him in a trust, and creeps
Beneath the folly this is day bereft
Of sound. But Peter is a man who strides
Among them with a speech to tell that dawn
Has made an end of tears. Women weep
With joy and cry His Galilee command:
And two who walked upon a road return
With breathless message of event: of Hands
Enfolding bread, and breaking it to fragments
At Emmaus while they watched His face,
And heard Him speaking in remembered words!

But day descends to night and they are closed
Behind the bolts and shutters of a room
Lest what they know, and what the day portends,
Be raised against them in the clubs of blunt
Rebellions. They are trembling in a fear
New mobs will come demanding surer tombs,
And stronger death, and wounds more deeply dug . . .

When He is standing in the midst of them
As One Who moves to children in the dark
And lifts a voice to quiet needless dreams.

"Peace be to you."

He offers them His hands and they have seen
The reddened seals in evidence of love;

They touch His hands, and then His opened side
With the great wound gleaming on the Heart of peace.

"As the Father hath sent me, I also send you."

With steady step He moves, and one by one
Their faces moisten in the living breath
Of Him Who hung upon the cross and died!

*"Receive ye the Holy Ghost. Whose sins you
shall forgive, they are forgiven them. . . ."*

They will be fortressed in this room again
And stand in sentry watch while Thomas kneels
Saluting in a pledge his Lord and God.
This cenacle shall be to them defense
And refuge, Temple, and a roof above
The wind and tongues of Pentecostal flame;
And yet the thrust of all they are to be
Across the ringing battles of our world
Has been already told in quickened breath
That touches them and makes them living swords.

*   *   *

Remaining time is swift uncertainty
They strive to lengthen in a clinging ache
For Him, and He consents to give them hills,
And skies, and presence on familiar shores
In Galilee. He brings them to the sands
And broils a fish, inviting them to eat:
Peter, wading, is an eager lunge
To shout above the waters that he comes. . . .
Then Peter hears of sheep that he must feed,
And even of the lambs that are his care.

He beckons and they find a road
They still remember. Branches carpeted

The dust that day, and they recall how shouts
And holiday in tumult hailed Him, King.
They seem reentered on triumphant ways
And hope of royal honors stirs anew.

He speaks command and they are listening,
He speaks: and they receive their waiting world.

"Ye men of Galilee, why stand you looking up . . . ?"

For Bethlehem has gone beyond the star,
And keeps with holy Nazareth a dear,
Eternal memory for God. His face
Is past the burning of our thousand suns,
And comets may not light to Him the search
That once was turning on the darkened Hill.
His voice is silence: He is instant plea:
His heart is haloed in an endless hope
"Unto the consummation of the world."

St. Ann's
Manlius, N. Y.
February 2, 1950

The chapter headings and all italicized words within the course of the narrative are exact quotations from the Scriptures. The passage from which the title derives is found in the new English translation of the Gospels by Ronald A. Knox.

J. W. L.

NIHIL OBSTAT: Vincent M. Mayer, O.F.M. Conv.
IMPRIMATUR: ✠ Walter A. Foery, Bishop of Syracuse, N.Y.
April 4, 1950, Syracuse, N.Y.